SLAVERY TO SUCCESS

A CHRISTIAN'S GUIDE TO UNWRAPPING GOD'S GIFT OF ABUNDANCE

DAN KAMMEYER

© **Copyright Dan Kammeyer 2021 - All rights reserved.**

The content contained within this book may not be reproduced, duplicated or transmitted without direct written permission from the author or the publisher.

Under no circumstances will any blame or legal responsibility be held against the publisher, or author, for any damages, reparation, or monetary loss due to the information contained within this book. Either directly or indirectly. You are responsible for your own choices, actions, and results.

Legal Notice:

This book is copyright protected. This book is only for personal use. You cannot amend, distribute, sell, use, quote or paraphrase any part, or the content within this book, without the consent of the author or publisher.

Disclaimer Notice:

Please note the information contained within this document is for educational and entertainment purposes only. All effort has been executed to present accurate, up to date, and reliable, complete information. No warranties of any kind are declared or implied. Readers acknowledge that the author is not engaging in the rendering of legal, financial, medical or professional advice. The content within this book has been derived from various sources. Please consult a licensed professional before attempting any techniques outlined in this book.

By reading this document, the reader agrees that under no circumstances is the author responsible for any losses, direct or indirect, which are incurred as a result of the use of the information contained within this document, including, but not limited to, — errors, omissions, or inaccuracies.

CONTENTS

Introduction — v

Part I
PART I: THE CASE FOR ABUNDANT LIVING

1. Does God Want Me to Be Wealthy? — 3
2. What is Money? — 11
3. What Does the Bible Say About Money? — 18
4. Can Money Really Buy Happiness? — 24

Part II
PART II: TAKING CONTROL OF YOUR FINANCIAL DESTINY

5. A World of Spiritual Laws — 29
6. Financial Education 101 — 36

JUST FOR YOU!

A FREE GIFT TO OUR READERS

3 better questions to start asking to level up your life right away!

Visit this link:

http://free.slaverytosuccess.com

INTRODUCTION

As a Christian, I understand that there are two types of wealth I should be concerned with; riches on earth and riches in heaven. Christ Himself explained that as believers, we should "store up treasures in heaven, where moth and rust do not destroy" (Matt 6:20) and that we can and should use earthly wealth to do so ("Go, sell everything you have and give to the poor, and you will have treasure in heaven." - Mark 10:21.) This is the subject I would like to expand upon in this book, as well as address some misconceptions regarding earthly wealth that seem to have become prevalent in the church today.

An unfortunate byproduct of our time spent on earth is a forced relationship with money that has great constructive - and destructive - potential. We've all heard the cliché that everyone must deal with "death and taxes." As followers of Christ, we could replace "taxes" with "money" because for many Christians, it's the source of their greatest frustration.

Let me be clear about what this book is not, however. I do not subscribe to the idea of "Prosperity Doctrine" that teaches a sort of "Christianity Lite" that's been watered down to appeal to the selfish desires of a consumerist society. I will not be discussing any "get rich quick" schemes or tell you what you should do with the money God has entrusted to you. I merely want to share what the Lord has laid on my heart to tell anyone who has been pressed into the world's financial mold of "earn and spend," which itself is the product of a system that (I think) seeks to limit Christianity's overall influence by paralyzing individual Christians financially.

You see, there is a great conspiracy enacted against the average person by the authorities and spiritual powers of this world. It is evidenced in the educational system we are indoctrinated with, as well as some of the lesser-known laws of the land. **The enemy knows that in the same way the quickest path to a man's heart can be through his stomach, the quickest way to his soul can be through his wallet.**

In short, my hope for this book is to help the reader overcome any apprehension toward developing their worldly influence they may have, as well as provide examples and ways of thinking that will assist in accomplishing whatever endeavors the Lord has placed them here to do. I hope that the reader is ready to hear what I have to say, and that I convey the ideas contained herein in a way that is easy to understand.

As a primer for what you are about to read, I would recommend going to the back of this book (page 50) and working through the "Asset and Liability" exercise *without looking at the answers*. Then when you have finished the book, go through the exercise again, and feel free to review the correct answers.

PART I: THE CASE FOR ABUNDANT LIVING

1

DOES GOD WANT ME TO BE WEALTHY?

I once heard a joke about a small child telling an adult family member, "God must really like poor people." The adult replied with a puzzled look on their face, "What makes you say that?" The small child exclaimed, "He made so many of them!" This simple observation has a significant undertone. Why are so many people poor? One of my mentors once told me that **people are not poor because they do not have money; they are poor because of the way they think**. When he first told me that, I admit that I really didn't understand what he meant by it. As a child of a single parent, I grew up in a household that would be considered poor in the statistical sense. Yet, since I never had any exposure to a life of abundance, I had no reason to *think* any differently. Such is the case with the vast majority of people in these circumstances. They are simply the product of their environment. To further reinforce my financial paralysis once I became an adult, my general perspective of wealthy people was that their money was proof that they were greedy and had exploited others to get ahead. I got this way of thinking from the other "poor" people I hung around with- a product of my association, which is a subject I will discuss in a later chapter. As I matured and became exposed to different ways of thinking, however, a different picture of earthly wealth came into focus.

If I were to ask random church members the question "Does God want you to be wealthy?" I would expect to get a variety of answers ranging from a reference to Mark 10:23, saying "Of course not! The Bible says it's harder for a rich person to get to heaven than it is for a camel to go through the eye of a needle!" all the way to, "Absolutely! Otherwise God wouldn't have given me such a desire to be rich!" As with so many controversial subjects in life, I really think the truth lies in the middle somewhere. A better question you might want to ask yourself is, "Does God want me to be *poor*?" I suppose the answer would depend on what I meant by "poor." Let's take a minute to develop that thought before going any further.

I've already mentioned that people are poor because of the way they think, not because of the status of their bank accounts. In the United States, the way this plays out is through our overwhelming tendency to be *consumers*. If the US had an official religion, I'm convinced that it would be "self-centered materialism." In plain terms, we are taught to spend whatever money we earn, and even spend money before we earn it (using credit.) As a worship leader, I've even seen this same mentality manifest itself in the way many churchgoers have become "consumers of worship." On Sundays, these people attend church for what they can "get out of it." In Romans 12:2, Paul talked about not letting the world press us into its mold. The unfortunate truth for a lot of Christians is that they get pressed into conformity at an early age because they don't see the mold for what it is! The fact of the matter is that the world trains us to be poor and middle class by teaching us to be consumers (how many credit cards does the average American have now?) and to depend on others (have you ever noticed that in school, we are all taught how to work for someone else, not how to run our own business?) It's this system that works against us in order to make us easier to manipulate. I know that's a bold statement, but think about it for a minute. Why else would there be such a small percentage (less than 5%) of households in America (the wealthiest country in human history) that are in control of their own financial future? By the way, the only difference between the poor and middle class is that a middle class individual has more consumer debt in the way of car loans, credit cards, etc. The point is that both types of people run out of money before they run out of month, and there is a correlation between our financial habits and our spiritual maturity (a subject I will discuss in a later chapter.)

Now that I've defined what I mean by "poor," I want to make it clear that if you fall into one of the categories described above, there is hope! Jesus did say that "Blessed are the poor in spirit, for theirs is the kingdom of heaven" (Matt 5:3.) Note that He did *not* say "Blessed are the poor in spirit, for they will stay that way forever." We all start poor when we first move out of our parents' house anyway, right? I don't think I've ever met a college student who didn't have money problems! It's a different story when a 30 or 40-year-old has the same financial issues, however! The important thing to remember is that being poor or middle class should be a temporary situation while you develop your financial security (not to be confused with job security.) **Being poor should be a starting point, not a permanent situation!**

At this point, I should probably define what I mean by "wealth" as well. Different people have different definitions for the term "wealth." Some define it by their total net worth. Others define it by the length of time they could stop working and still live comfortably. I think of wealth as having financial security, in that you know that income will continue to flow into your household regardless of your efforts, combined with control of your own time and financial destiny, all of which really boils down to having the power of choice. Let me give you an example: If I want to drive the safest car available for my family to ride in, I want to be able to base my buying decision on that, instead of what my job dictates that I can afford. Does that make sense? **Our tendency is to settle for less simply because the choices we made yesterday limit the**

choices we get to make today. Ask anyone who bought a sub-prime loan during the real estate bubble of the late 2000s, and they will understand what I mean by that statement.

Let's get back to the question at hand. Does God want us to be wealthy? We certainly have an argument against Him wanting us to be poor. Let's go back to what Jesus said in Mark 10:23: It's easier for a camel to go through the eye of a needle than it is for a rich person to get into heaven. On the surface, it may appear as if He is inferring that it's next to impossible for someone who's rich to go to heaven. I don't think that's what He was saying, though. In Matthew Henry's commentary on this passage, he mentions that "those who eagerly seek the wealth of the world will never correctly prize Christ and His grace." I really think that's a more accurate description of what Jesus was trying to convey. The Bible is loaded with references to money and wealth (which we will analyze in chapter 3), and they all have a common thread; that you really do have to ultimately choose what to put your trust in: Christ or money. And the more you put your faith in one, the more it dwindles toward the other. I think Jesus was commenting on how a majority of the people who accumulate wealth do so out of either fear or greed, rather than out of wisdom and good stewardship. Otherwise people like King Solomon, Abraham, and Job would have been painted very differently in Scripture. Not to mention all the people who have come to know the Lord after they were already wealthy.

Okay, so we know God doesn't want us to be poor, and we know it's not sinful to be wealthy. What arguments, if any, are there *for* God wanting us to be wealthy? I think the main reason the average Christian would have a hard time answering that question is because they don't personally know a wealthy Christian. Here's the quick answer: God can use you more when you have more resources at your disposal! I think now would be a good time for me to share an observation with you that you may find offensive. Please know that it isn't my intention to offend anyone with this next statement! What I have found through my interactions with Christians that have abundance and those who do not, is that the ones who have little wealth generally tend to be *more* selfish with their resources than those who have abundance. This is probably because people who trade hours for dollars at a job associate money with scarcity. This is due to the hard work they had to trade for it, as well as the inherent limitations of doing so (we only have so many hours to trade.) On the other hand, those who live a life of abundance have a different view of their resources. One of my wealthy friends once told me that **money is a lot like air: you only think about it when you don't have enough of it.** Subsequently, he has been willing and able to fund almost every major undertaking his church has pursued in recent years.

Before I go any further, let me address what some of you may be thinking. "What about the parable about the widow giving her last bit of money and how her offering was of more value than all the money the rich guys were throwing into the offering?" I am of course referring to Mark 12:41-44. Once again, on the surface it appears as if Jesus is denouncing the good works of the rich, but as usual, there is a deeper meaning if we look closer. Remember, Jesus knows our hearts! The rich people in question were not giving out of love for God and his ministry, but rather to further their public image by making a big deal out of how much money they were putting into the offering plate. The widow, however, was giving out of a combination of love for the Lord and faith in his ability to provide for her needs. Which leads me to an important fact about my wealthy friend- all the giving he does, he does so *anonymously*. Don't get me wrong. I'm not saying all affluent Christians have pure motives. You will always have impostors, but there are ways of sorting them out (Matthew 6:3 says "But when you give to the needy, do not let your left hand know what your right hand is doing.")

I want to make one very important point before moving on. My wealthy friend, and most of the Godly men and women who live abundant lives today, started in the same place as the widow in the Bible with barely a few pennies to rub together! They too acted out of faith when they had nothing, and proved to God that they could be trusted with more. That's really the only difference between them and someone who has yet to develop their financial resources.

I don't know about you, but I would rather be the anonymous donor that God was able to use to construct a new church building, or fund a mission trip to Africa. I would not want to be a "consumer of worship" my whole life! If that isn't a good argument toward stepping out in faith and committing to developing your earthly resources, I don't know what is. Just remember that **when God trusts us with more, he expects us to improve our standard of giving, not our standard of living!**

2

WHAT IS MONEY?

In the introduction, I mentioned that part of my motivation for writing this book was to address some common misconceptions with regards to earthly wealth. The subject of money has become so controversial that I think most people just try to avoid it altogether instead of learning what it is and how it works. The truth of the matter is that unless you learn about money and how to control it, it will ultimately control your choices instead. The sad part is that the educational system we are all indoctrinated into does very little to teach us about the true nature of the financial system we have to participate in, and I think it's on purpose.

Why Money Was Invented

Before the rise of human civilization, there was no real need for a monetary system. Resources were shared by everyone in the small communities they lived in and everyone's needs were met. Once small communities became larger, though, trading products or services directly became obsolete. What if the person who has what I want isn't interested in what I can offer in trade? A system that provided a common medium of exchange was necessary. The answer to that need was the invention of money in the form of gold or silver coins. The monetary system would allow me to trade my product or service to someone who does want it in exchange for a universally accepted medium. Then I could use that to trade for a product or service that I want. It's a simple concept that our civilization has built upon for thousands of years. Over time, governments wanted to centralize (and therefore more closely control) their reserves of precious metals, so they moved to a paper currency that took the place of circulating the actual gold and silver. At any time, an individual was able to exchange the paper currency for the equivalent amount of gold or silver from the treasury, though. As the population grew, however, there was increased demand for money, but not enough gold to back it all, so governments started relaxing the requirement to have enough gold on hand to exchange for the currency. The mentality was that not everyone would want to exchange their currency for gold at one time anyway. Then came the globalization of the economy. As countries began trading with each other, the reserves of certain countries would get depleted because other countries would exchange the currency they accumulated via trade, and then exchange it for gold from that government's treasury. This had the effect of weakening the reserves (and subsequent buying power) of whatever country was subjected to the siphoning effect. This led to the *fiat* system we have today. That means that there is no longer a direct connection between the currency and a commodity that has intrinsic value (like gold.) I would encourage you to research this subject further on your own, as my summary here only scratches the surface of this topic.

The Dollar Bill Is Not Money (Anymore)

As of 1971, you can no longer exchange your dollars for gold or silver from the US Treasury. What that means is that those dollar bills in your wallet (you do have some, right?) are not actually *money* anymore. They're actually just a *fiat currency*. A dollar bill is just a piece of dirty paper and has no intrinsic value, except for the purchasing power it has been mandated to have by the government (which is what fiat means.) Basically, that means our currency is only usable as long as the government that issued it exists and has power to enforce it. If you don't believe me, think of what would happen if the US government collapsed tomorrow. I guarantee if you have a stash of gold or silver coins, you'd still be able to buy food and clothing with them, but the chances of anyone (especially foreign entities) taking paper US dollars would be slim to none. This very thing happened after the American Civil War, when Confederate money became completely worthless.

Money Can Be Created Out of Thin Air

Now that you understand that the dollars we have become so attached to are not actually money, you can let go of the idea that they are a scarce commodity, and that there is only one big pie that everyone gets a slice of. That's the reason the average person thinks wealthy people are "greedy." They think that since there's just one big pie that everyone shares, that means when someone has a bigger slice, someone else has to get a smaller one. That is simply not true! Wealthy people just make more pies! They create money out of nothing. Let me give you an example to explain what I mean by that. Let's say you bought a house that's in foreclosure today for $50,000. Now let's say you clean it up, maybe put some new carpet in it, and then someone offers to buy it from you for $75,000 next week. Where did that $25,000 of "equity appreciation" come from? Did the US government run to the printing press and print off another $25,000 of paper currency so you could have that extra money? Nope. It was created out of thin air! The same thing happens in the stock market every day when stock prices rise due to increased demand. You see, the vast majority of wealth in the world is actually being created in the various banks' computer databases versus being printed on paper by the Federal Reserve. The reason it's important that you understand this dynamic is to get past the idea that in order for you to accumulate earthly abundance, you need to have a high-paying job or inherit a large sum of money. The opportunity to create money out of nothing is available to everyone! Now that I've taken some time to talk about what money *isn't*, let's discuss what money really is.

Money is a Temporal Tool

When you look at it from an eternal perspective, money is really just a tool that we use temporarily while we're here on earth ("Cast but a glance at riches, and they are gone, for they will surely sprout wings and fly off to the sky like an eagle." Proverbs 23:5). What's tragic is how many of us work most of our lives for money, effectively becoming slaves to it as mentioned in Romans 6:16 ("Don't you realize that you become the slave of whatever you choose to obey?") instead of making our money work for us (which is what a tool is supposed to do.)

Money is an Amplifier of Character

In the last chapter I mentioned how earthly resources give one the privilege of being the benefactor of various Kingdom-building endeavors. This is really just one example of how a good person will do good things with money. Likewise, you can expect a bad person to do bad things with money (Al Capone would be a good example.) Money has no personality; it takes on the personality of the person who holds it.

Money Gives Its Owner the Power of Choice

Let's face it; living in the US is expensive. It costs money to eat, to sleep (somewhere safe), to have relationships, you name it. It even costs money to die (in the form of estate taxes.) What's tragic about most people's lives is that *what* they eat, *where* they sleep, *who* they are friends with, and possibly even *how* they die are dictated by someone else. Let me explain. If every car in the world had the exact same price tag, would you still be driving the same one as you are today? There might be a couple people out there that would say "yes," but I'm willing to bet that the vast majority of you would not. You had to select from the cars that you could afford, right? When you think about it, if price wasn't a factor, you would be able to buy a car based on how safe it is for your family to ride in it instead of its fuel efficiency or some other economic factor. The same probably goes for the house you sleep in, the restaurants you frequent and the health care program you're enrolled in. I mention these things to bring to your attention the lack of real control most people have over the decisions they make in their lives. The fact of the matter is that their options are limited by the amount of money their job pays them.

Keep in mind that a job doesn't pay a person what *they* are worth, but rather what the *position* is worth to the employer. It's not a conspiracy against the working class of America or anything; it's just how businesses operate. If every company paid everyone what they were worth, they'd all go bankrupt! Don't get me wrong; I'm not against jobs. The world needs teachers, waiters, salespeople and such. I just think most people expect a job to deliver more than it's really designed to give. Robert Kiyosaki explained it best when he said that **a job is "a temporary solution to a long-term problem**" (referring to an individual's need for regular income to support their basic needs before and after retirement.) In other words, there really isn't a built-in exit strategy for them anymore. In the Industrial Age (late 1800s to 1974), most people had the same job for 40 years and then they retired with a pension, which was included with their employment contract. That all changed in 1974 when Congress passed ERISA- the Employee Retirement Income Security Act, which created the 401k plans we are all forced to use today. While this law was spun to the American public as being in their best interests, the truth is that ERISA was actually passed to benefit *employers* by reducing their responsibility (and inherent expenses) for their employees' retirement needs. I don't really want to go too far into this subject, but if you want to read more about it, I would suggest reading Rich Dad's Prophecy by Robert Kiyosaki.

3

WHAT DOES THE BIBLE SAY ABOUT MONEY?

Would you believe Scripture actually mentions financial matters more often than the subjects of healing, mercy, and even prayer? You will find the general subject of money covered 140 times throughout the Bible. In addition to those passages, gold is specifically referenced 417 times, and silver 320 times. Needless to say, God has a lot to say when it comes to this subject! I'm sure an entire book could be dedicated to examining those verses, but I just want to highlight a few fundamental truths that the Lord has laid out in His Word.

Earthly Wealth and Heavenly Wealth Are Not the Same

In Luke 16:19-31, Jesus tells a parable that makes it clear that you do not need to be wealthy on earth to have riches in heaven. The two are not mutually exclusive, however, as most Christians are in the habit of thinking. In Matthew 6:24, Jesus says "No one can serve two masters…You cannot serve both God and money." Notice the last sentence of that verse: "You cannot *serve* both God and money" (emphasis added.) In the last chapter, I mentioned how a lot of people spend their lives working for (serving) money instead of making it serve them. Once we learn how to be good stewards of the resources God has entrusted to us, I'm convinced that we will then have the opportunity to develop both material and heavenly wealth at the same time.

The *Love* of Money is the Root of All Evil

This has to be one of the most misquoted Bible verses ever. I am, of course, talking about 1Timothy 6:10. The way it is usually quoted is that "money is the root of all evil." It's amazing how omitting just a single word can completely change the fundamental meaning of such a powerful statement. **Money is not inherently good or evil. It takes on the character of the one who holds it!** A much more difficult verse to manipulate would be Matthew 6:33: "…seek first his kingdom and his righteousness, and all these things will be given to you as well." This verse implies that one can have abundance on earth and in heaven as long as you are serving God, and you aren't "possessed by your possessions." In Jeremiah 29:11, God even specifically states that he wants us to be prosperous: "'For I know the plans I have for you,' declares the Lord, 'plans to *prosper* you and not to harm you, plans to give you hope and a future'" (emphasis added.) Then again in John 10:10: "...I came that they may have life, and have it *abundantly*" (emphasis added again.) The point I'm trying to make is that if we are serving God with our money instead of being subservient to it like we are all taught to be, there's really no reason not to expect a life of abundance (financial security.)

He Who Has Will Be Given More (Because of His Habits)

I think it's really important to get past the idea that people with material wealth somehow "got lucky" or they were born into it. In my opinion, this mode of thinking is really just a thinly veiled excuse for being too lazy to pursue something better. The truth is that the vast majority of millionaires in the US are first-generation wealthy, and they didn't become millionaires until late in their lives. That means that they have developed their personal fortunes throughout the course of their life, and did not inherit any of it. They didn't get a lucky break at all. They just realized that the same spiritual rules of success (which we will cover in a later chapter) apply to everyone. When you take these things into account, it becomes clear that **the only difference**

between a poor person and a wealthy person is how they use their time, energy, and money!

Jesus elaborated on the connection between our habits and our financial situation in Matthew 25:14-30 with the parable of the talents. Let's start by looking at verse 15: "To one he gave five talents, to another two, and to another one, each *according to his ability*" (emphasis added.) The first point worth making is that when the master trusted the money to the servants, he knew that they each had different habits when it came to managing finances. While this parable is traditionally interpreted to refer to spiritual gifts, the same concept is easily applied to material resources. If we want the Lord to trust us with more influence here on earth, there are some questions we should be asking ourselves. Do my habits prove to God that he can trust me with more? Do I spend everything I earn? Do I set aside a portion of my income to dedicate to the Lord's purposes? Have I developed a level of discipline necessary to be a good steward of what he's already trusted me with? Don't worry if your financial discipline is still a work in progress; it is for everyone. The whole purpose of this book is to help you develop the knowledge and habits necessary to develop your financial "maturity" in a positive way.

Verse 16 reinforces the idea that money is meant to be a tool that works for us instead of the other way around: "The one who had received five talents went off right away and *put his money to work* and gained five more" (emphasis added.) I think it's worth mentioning that this is the guy the master gave the most money to in the first place, probably because he knew he was the most financially educated of the group. I also think it's interesting that it mentions that he went out "right away" and did something with it. He knew the time to act was right then, with no procrastination. The servant who was given two talents was also successful in multiplying his wealth (using the same techniques), but the one who was trusted with the least amount (because of his poor habits in the first place) hid the money out of fear. There are just two more points I would like to make from this passage. First, when the master returned, he praised both of the servants that were good stewards of the money he gave them. The actual amount that was gained wasn't important to the master, just that they made the money work for them. Secondly, the primary motivation for the third servant's actions was fear (verse 25 – "I was afraid and went out and hid your gold in the ground.") I think fear is what keeps the vast majority of Christians from actively developing their financial education. Fear of temptation, fear of taking risk, fear of loss, fear of what they don't understand. I'd like to point out that when the master learned that the servant hid the money out of fear, he called the servant *lazy* (verse 26) and gave his talent to the one who had been given 5 already. In other words, if we don't purposely develop our financial habits, it may be due to laziness! I don't know about you, but I'd rather spend my time, energy, and money becoming more like the first servant in the parable, as opposed to the last one- which is what we will become by default. Remember, you cannot coast uphill. I cannot stress this point enough: **developing wealthy habits only happens on purpose. If you don't, poor habits will develop automatically.**

4

CAN MONEY REALLY BUY HAPPINESS?

You've probably heard phrases like these before:

"Money can't buy happiness- look at all the miserable famous people we see on TV every day!"

"Being rich doesn't make you happy, but being poor doesn't make you happy either!"

"Money can't buy happiness, but it can buy jet skis, and every person I've ever seen on a jet ski had a smile on their face!"

In all seriousness, the general consensus is that having large amounts of money in and of itself does not make anyone happy.

Likewise, however, the lack of large amounts of money has the exact same bearing on one's happiness. John Maxwell once said, "Happiness is growth." I really can't think of a better way to put it. Notice that no mention of money is made or even insinuated. My experience has taught me that the money we typically associate with an affluent person's happiness is actually just a byproduct of the character growth that was required to attain it. Those of us who can't seem to "get ahead" financially look at others who live abundantly and our first instinct is to assume they received their material wealth in a lump sum, like a lottery. Nothing could be further from the truth, however. In fact, the vast majority of people who do win the lottery are back to being poor again within a few short years. Why do you suppose that is? I'm convinced it's because most people who win the lottery never develop their financial maturity past being the hyper-consumer that we are all conditioned to be by society. We are taught (subconsciously) that if we HAVE some material possession, we will DO things that will in turn make us BE happy. An example would a beer commercial that shows some average Joe who picks up a drink, and all the sudden girls come out of nowhere and he is surrounded by a party that appeared out of thin air. This psychology is used to sell everything from body spray to energy drinks to car tires. Here's the thing; what we are conditioned to think is actually the exact opposite of what it takes to really be happy! The reality is that in order to be happy in this life, we need to grow our character so that we will BE good stewards of the resources God has blessed us with. A growing person will DO the right things with money (by making it work for them), and as a result they will HAVE more resources and the choices that come with it. If you only learn one thing from this entire book, the most valuable concept would be to recognize that in order to be happy, the process outlined above must happen in the following order:

Be>Do>Have

Understand that your character is the greatest asset you have. No one can take it from you, and it is the only thing you take with you when you leave this earth. Invest in your personal growth and you will not be disappointed. To aid you in this process, the remainder of this book will focus on developing your understanding of the spiritual laws at work around us, as well as providing a starting point for your financial education.

PART II: TAKING CONTROL OF YOUR FINANCIAL DESTINY

5

A WORLD OF SPIRITUAL LAWS

I don't think anyone would argue that we live in a world governed by laws. Not just civil laws established by our society, but physical and spiritual laws as well. Examples of physical laws would include the laws of gravity, magnetism, and motion. "Spiritual Laws," while getting a lot less mainstream attention, have just as much control over what happens to us in life as the physical ones, but their principles are only practically applied by a small percentage of the populace. More importantly, **understanding and abiding by these laws can make the difference between a life of abundance and a life of scarcity**. This won't be a complete list by any means, but I will do my best to cover the three that I have found to be most important on my journey toward living a prosperous and successful life, as promised in Joshua 1:8 ("Keep this Book of the Law always on your lips; meditate on it day and night, so that you may be careful to do everything written in it. Then you will be prosperous and successful.")

The Law of Reciprocity (Sowing and Reaping)

There are numerous references to this law in scripture, but Galatians 6:7 is the most exact: "Whatever a man sows, that he will also reap." Put simply, this law states that if someone sows money, they will reap money. If they sow time, they will reap time. If they sow evil, they will reap evil. Non-Christians typically refer to this as "Karma" and have a basic understanding of how it operates. While I'd known of this principle for quite a few years, I didn't really understand its full impact until relatively recently in my life. I have been sowing my time by serving in the worship ministry at various churches for numerous years, but I confess that I was only sporadically contributing financially. When I made the shift in my career from employee to being self-employed a while back, my income level dropped significantly, but I was only working about one forth the amount of hours as before in any given week. One day, it finally hit me that I had reaped time in return for all the time I had sowed in service to the church! Once I had fully grasped that idea, I began faithfully giving monetarily as well, and the Lord has blessed us with a harvest of material resources as a result. It really is just that simple. Donating your time, energy, and material resources to God's ministry is an example of sowing, with a guarantee of return from the Lord himself ("Bring the whole tithe into the storehouse, that there may be food in my house. Test me in this," says the LORD Almighty, "and see if I will not throw open the floodgates of heaven and pour out so much blessing that there will not be room enough to store it." Malachi 3:10!) Another example of sowing one's time would be all the effort the owner of the company you work for put into creating the system that defines the organization's operation. All the work that was required to start the company only had to be done once, but it continues to pay the owner on a regular basis. This is in direct contrast to a job, which requires continuous effort to maintain a constant income. Which brings me to an interesting question: are you "sowing" your time at a job? Most jobs require an individual to give their employer 40 of the best hours of their week, but they never get time back in return. They are getting a salary or an hourly wage. In reality, they are simply exchanging one commodity (time and energy) for another (money.) This, by definition, is *not* sowing. That is why a job isn't designed to really get anyone ahead in life. Do you see the difference? The owner invested (sowed) their time, energy, and money into something that would reap the same things later on in the form of not having to work a 40 hour a week job in order to generate a constant income. They may only have to work 10 hours a week or so to manage the company they started, or they could pay someone else to manage it for them and have complete control over their time!

The same rules apply for money. There are countless ways individuals can sow their money (apart from donating it) by investing in things that reap a harvest. Examples would include investment real estate, high-yield stocks, limited partnerships, gold and silver, and intellectual properties. If there are so many opportunities to invest our resources, why don't more people do it? I think there are a number of reasons, but the most important one is that we aren't taught to! Like I mentioned earlier in the book, we are all taught from an early age by our society to be consumers- to trade hours for dollars, then trade those dollars for liabilities (I'll define what liabilities really are in the next chapter.) A person with habits like that is "like a wave of the sea, blown and tossed by the wind" (James 1:6.) Their buying habits are defined by whatever the latest fad is, and they have little hope of developing any sense of discipline until they change their ways. It is my hope that this book will encourage anyone who is in this situation to break free of this financial mold that the world has pressed them into, and to offer the basic education needed to begin the process.

The Power of Association

Did your parents try to control who your best friends were when you were growing up? I remember my mother would always want to meet any new friend I wanted to spend time with, as well as their parents. Now that I'm a parent, I understand why she did that: it was because she understood the power of association. The simplest way I've heard it expressed is that "**you will become like the people you spend the most time with**." It is very important that we make a conscious effort to spend more time with people who are encouraging, uplifting, positive, and have more mature habits than we do for this reason ("The way of fools seems right to them, but the wise listen to advice." Proverbs 12:15.) Some ways this could be accomplished would be to read books written by individuals who have already proven their character by their accomplishments, making new friends at church, or volunteering your time with a local community outreach organization (which are usually operated by individuals who are not as self-centered as most.) This also means that we need to limit our time spent with people who exhibit the habits we do not want to cultivate. Paul mentions this in 1 Corinthians 5:11 ("I am writing to you that you must not associate with anyone who claims to be a brother or sister but is sexually immoral or greedy, an idolater or slanderer, a drunkard or swindler. Do not even eat with such people.") Proverbs 13:20 ("Walk with the wise and become wise, for a companion of fools suffers harm.") also mentions how your association determines your destiny. I realize this may mean that the company you keep will need to change, which I understand is tough to do, especially if you work with some of the people you shouldn't be hanging around with. Everyone's situation is a little different, but I can tell you one of the best steps you can take in this regard is to select a mentor (maybe a pastor or business leader) to help you through the necessary changes- and let me make it very clear that it *is* necessary. **You simply cannot live a life of abundance if you are surrounded by scarcity!**

The Power of the Spoken Word

We can see this law at work all the way back in the Bible's depiction of the creation of the world. Starting in Genesis 1:3 ("And God said, "Let there be light," and there was light"), God creates each aspect of our universe individually by *speaking* them into existence! Unbeknownst to most people, our words also have very real creative (and destructive) power. Because of our ignorance, however, this power is usually used against us. Many years ago, I attended a training class on communication that taught us how to control how we phrase certain things. In a situation that required us to do extra work, we were taught to say "I'll be happy to..." Instead of "I'll have to..." The reasoning being that what we say actually affects our subconscious mind and its disposition toward how we feel about performing that specific task. If we eliminate the "I'll have to" speak and replace it with "I'll be happy to," we will actually develop a desire to do whatever it is we're talking about. In reality, we are "programming" our subconscious mind by what we say every day, whether we know it or not! All it takes to use this very powerful tool in your favor is to control what you say, and make sure that you speak positively about yourself in general. I don't mean that you should sound arrogant, but **it is important to try to see yourself the way God sees you instead of the way the world may see you**. Keep in mind that our words are a derivative of our thoughts ("the mouth speaks what the heart is full of" Matthew 12:34), and our thoughts are completely within our control. As long as we take our thoughts captive, making sure that we dump the negative ones and keep the positive ones ("we take captive every thought to make it obedient to Christ" 2 Corinthians 10:5), we will move toward maturity. Just remember that your thoughts determine your words and actions, which in turn define your habits, which determine your character, which ultimately dictates your destiny! For more in-depth information on this subject, I would recommend reading <u>Think and Grow Rich</u> by Napoleon Hill and <u>Grow Rich While You Sleep</u> by Ben Sweetland.

Understanding the three principles outlined above will go a long way toward helping you be successful in this world, regardless of your endeavors. Just know that success is a team sport, and therefore requires you to learn how to interact with others in a positive way that benefits everyone involved. Just know that none of this happens overnight, and while the Lord won't give you more than you can handle, keep in mind that he won't give you more resources than you can handle maturely either!

6

FINANCIAL EDUCATION 101

There are actually four main categories of education in this world. The last chapter covered some basics with regards to one of these categories, and this chapter will focus on another. The primary categories of education (as I see it) are:

- ACADEMIC
- SPIRITUAL
- PROFESSIONAL
- FINANCIAL

Academic education includes the general studies each of us went through during our years in school. Examples would be reading, writing, and basic mathematics. Academic education is a foundational requirement to learning some of the more advanced subjects related to the other 3 categories of learning. It would be very difficult to develop one's knowledge of the Bible, for instance, if one could not read it in the first place! A lot of people think once they are out of school, all the learning is over and they can finally go out into the real world and start making money by applying what they learned. The truth, however, is that most of the learning still lies ahead of them as they develop the other three categories of education. This is yet another reason why only a small percentage of the general population is ever "successful" in real life. Someone can be an excellent academic student and still fail miserably in the real world. Have you ever heard of a banker ever asking to see someone's report card before offering them a loan? The point I'm trying to make is that it's only the individuals who recognize the need to mature themselves in all 4 categories (and do something about it) that move on to greater influence.

Spiritual education is also foundational, in my opinion, because it is from this category that we should draw our core values that we then apply to our professional and financial endeavors. That is why I decided to cover the subject of spiritual laws before moving on to the basics of financial education. Someone once told me that **the people who know *how* always work for the people who know *why***. If you aren't already developing this aspect of your education, some suggestions to begin would be to start a "read the Bible in one year" program, start attending a home Bible study, attend a local church regularly, and begin using a daily devotional resource. I think it's worth mentioning that none of the above recommendations require any financial expenditure, only an investment of time, which we all have!

Professional education includes all the skills and knowledge necessary to perform a specific occupation successfully. This type of education varies widely depending on the career path chosen. For example, a doctor requires many more years of college-level schooling, as well as years of experience as a resident. This is because the quality of their skills determines the health and well-being of other people who are dependent on their services. Other occupations require significantly less training to be performed in a satisfactory manner, because far less is at stake if they fail in their duties.

It is financial education that separates those who have and those who do not in this world. Sadly, it is this category of knowledge that is most lacking in our society. Even worse, I'm convinced that it's like that on purpose. As the United States industrialized a century ago, the primary source of capital shifted from land to labor. In order to maintain a constant labor supply, our educational system only teaches the citizenry how to be employees- how to be capital for someone else. It is the individuals who take it upon themselves (since no public institution is really teaching the subject) to develop their "financial literacy" that ultimately end up sowing their time, energy, and money instead of simply exchanging it their whole lives. It is my heartfelt belief that if you invest in your financial education, you too can begin to break free from the bondage that the world so readily presses us into by default. Since you can't take a course on financial security at your local college, where should you start your education on this subject? A great place to start would be to utilize the power of association described in the previous chapter. There are many books written by individuals who have already walked the path of abundance, and were willing to share the education they developed to do so. As a starting point, I would recommend Robert Kiyosaki's Rich Dad Poor Dad, followed by The Richest Man in Babylon by George Clason. These provide a great foundation for financial literacy, as well as motivation to change your financial situation.

Keep in mind that **there are two necessary ingredients to anyone's success; preparation and opportunity**. As I mentioned earlier in the book, there are numerous opportunities for sowing one's time and money. All that remains is to develop your understanding of how and where to do it! The best way to accomplish anything of worth is to know where you are now, decide where you want to end up, and then plot a course to get there. I'm going to explain this process by walking through what's called a Financial Statement. You can think of it as a couple different things. First off, it's like a "financial report card" for a company or a household. Secondly, it can be used as a sort of map to show you where changes need to be made in order to slowly make your current financial situation eventually look like your target one.

How to Read a Financial Statement

We are going to take a tour of all the components that make up a Financial Statement, as well as explain ways to shift your habits toward sowing instead of exchanging along the way. If you were to look up the financials of a publicly traded company on the Internet, you would find that it is broken up into two basic sections; an Income Statement and a Balance Sheet. Each of those sections is made up of two columns. The Income Statement has an Income section and an Expenses section. The Balance Sheet has an Assets section and a Liabilities section (see the diagram below.)

The Income Statement

In the context of a household, an Income Statement would be the same thing as a monthly budget. It's common knowledge that the first step to taking control of one's money is to monitor the way it flows in and out of their control. **The reason so**

many people run out of money before they run out of month is because they do not control their money; to an extent, it controls them. There are two basic parts to an Income Statement: an Income column, and an Expenses column. For most people, the Income column is populated by the monthly wages earned by the adults in the household. What most people do not know, however, is that there are actually 3 categories of income according to our country's tax laws, and each type is taxed differently. Just understanding the differences between the types of income can have a significant impact on your long-term financial situation. The three different types of income are:

- EARNED INCOME
- PORTFOLIO INCOME
- PASSIVE INCOME

You're probably already very familiar with earned income. This is any money that comes into your household as a direct result of your ongoing efforts. Basically any hours that you traded for dollars would fall into this category. It's also pretty well known that this is the type of income that the government taxes the most! It is extremely important that you understand that people who live a life of abundance do not earn a majority of their income in this category! You only have so many hours available to you, so exchanging hours for dollars always has a limit to the amount of resources it can generate. If hours were like seeds, this would be the equivalent of selling the seeds for a limited upfront profit instead of planting the seeds to get a much higher return in the future! **One of the reasons people do not "get ahead" in life is because they place a higher priority on immediate gratification than on long-term prosperity**.

Portfolio income is any money generated from financial investments. In other words, this is income that is not dependent on your direct efforts, but is instead produced by making money work for you. Examples of this type of income would be dividends or capital gains from stocks, or interest from any loans you make to others (like bonds or Certificates of Deposit.) This category of income is not taxed as highly as earned income, nor is it dependent on the number of hours someone has available, so there is no upper limit to the amount of reward it can generate. This is a great starting point for learning how to invest (sow) your resources instead of just consuming them. There is risk involved with investing, however, and I recommend finding mentorship and starting small if you choose to pursue this route. Like anything, risk can be minimized and sometimes mitigated through proper training and experience.

Passive income is really the goal for anyone wanting to live a life of abundance. Pretty much anyone we associate with mature wealth generates most of their income in this category. Business owners like Donald Trump, best-selling authors like Tom Clancy, and the statistic majority of all millionaires in the

United States utilize this category of income to develop their wealth. It's no coincidence that passive income is also the least taxed by the government. **It is by learning what it takes to invest your time, energy, and monetary resources into developing your passive income that will determine your family's financial destiny!** To give you a starting point, I'll list a few examples of methods to produce passive income: writing a book and collecting royalties, starting a part-time business (like a network marketing company) to generate residual commissions, purchasing a house to rent out for more than its mortgage payment, or entering into a limited partnership with a current business owner for a portion of their profits. These are all ways to generate a positive cash-flow that is not dependent on your on-going efforts.

At this point, it might make sense to provide some context for the previous paragraphs by giving a brief explanation of what Capitalism really is. Our economy is really nothing more than a series of interconnected business systems (companies.) Each system requires four different types of people that really fall into three basic categories, which I have outlined graphically below:

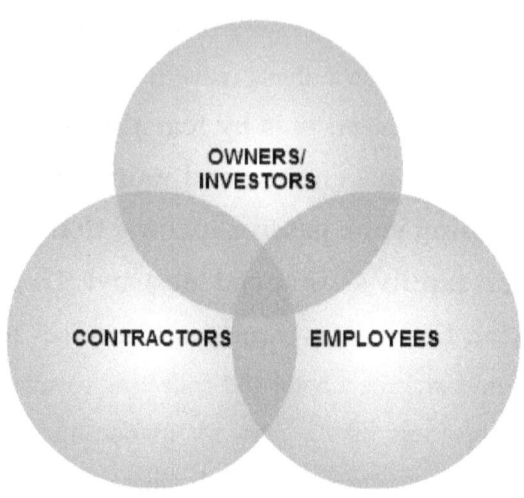

Companies are owned by individuals who invested their time, energy, and money into creating and developing the business system. The business system, in turn, provides passive income back to its owners and investors in the form of dividends and profits. Employees operate the system put in place by the owners, and contractors are used for services that the company would prefer not to pay an employee to do full time (like a lawyer or tax accountant.) Employees and contractors are compensated for their labor contributions and nothing more. They haven't *risked* anything for the purpose of furthering the company's interests, and therefore do not directly benefit from its success. Recognizing this relationship can provide some perspective on why there is no such thing as "corporate loyalty" in our society. Many employees that lose their jobs feel like they were treated unfairly somehow, when in reality the jobs were never really theirs to begin with. They were the company's. The point I'm trying to make is that **in order to have financial security, you have to stop looking for job security, for the two are mutually exclusive**. It's only by moving from the employee and contractor circles to the owner and investor circle that you truly get control of your financial destiny. In summary, your goal for the Income portion of your Financial Statement should be to constantly increase the amount generated by Portfolio and Passive income, while constantly reducing the amount generated by Earned income.

The Expense portion of the Income Statement is a little more straight-forward. A new term that you should add to your vocabulary is "cash-flow." It's sometimes referred to as "disposable income," but that is a term that was coined from a consumer mentality perspective. The idea is to maximize your monthly positive cash-flow (the amount of money you have left over after all your expenses) by reducing your Expense column as much as possible, while simultaneously increasing your Income column through the development of passive income streams. This may include reducing how much you spend on luxuries like eating out and entertainment, or paying off bad debt (which I will define later.) A great recommendation I can give you is to use a 10-10-80 rule for how you spend your monthly earnings. The first 10 represents you giving 10% of your monthly budget back to God in the form of a tithe or some sort of charitable giving that furthers his kingdom. By doing that, you will gain a great sense of power over your instinct to consume. It will help develop the understanding that what you have is not really yours, but God's, and that you are being trusted to be a good steward with those resources. The next 10% should be dedicated to the development of real assets. This portion should either go toward purchasing high-yield securities, or saved up to purchase investment real estate, or any other method that puts the money to work for you or generate some kind of Return On Investment (ROI.) The idea is to channel that money into something that will ultimately generate passive income either immediately or later on down the road. The remaining 80% is the money that you should base your standard of living on, and you can feel free to consume it as you please. It's God's will for us to live life to the fullest and in moderation, and spending habits based on these guidelines can accomplish both. Regardless of how tight your budget is, the first step to doing this is to write it all down (I've included a sample Financial Statement at the back of the book to give you a starting point.) Create a written budget either on paper or using a spreadsheet so you can visualize how money flows through your household. While we're on the subject of expenses, I'd like to make you aware of the 4 greatest enemies to developing positive cash flow. They are commonly referred to as the "four I's:"

- INCOME TAX
- INFLATION
- INTEREST
- INSURANCE

These are four types of expenses that will always continue to increase over time. You can think of these as four competitors for the money you are attempting to generate. It is important to factor each of these into any large financial decision you make Factoring these into your decision-making process will give you a better picture of whether the venture will be worth it or not. Let me give you some examples to illustrate my point. When I was serving in the United States Marine Corps, I can remember getting a promotion from Corporal (E-4) to Sergeant (E-5) and looking forward to a significant pay increase as a result. The reality, however, was the opposite! Because the additional income put me into a different income tax bracket, my pay was less than it was when my income was lower! That's definitely something worth examining before pursuing a different, higher-paying position at your job.

Inflation is probably the most obvious of the four, in that we can see prices going up all the time when we go to the supermarket. While the prices of technology products (like computers and cell phones) usually go down over time, it's the basic commodities like food and fuel that we see on a steady rise. What most people don't recognize is that every time the price of gas goes up, and your paycheck doesn't follow suit, you are actually getting a pay *cut*! We used to be able to put money in a savings account and let compound interest grow it for us faster than inflation, but now it takes a much greater return to outpace it enough to be worth it (which is why it's a better idea to put money into high-yield securities instead.)

An example of how interest and insurance work against you would be when you buy a car from a dealer. When you finance a car (make payments on it), the bank not only charges thousands of dollars in interest on the loan, but it also requires you to have full insurance coverage on the vehicle for the duration of the loan (usually about 5 years.) If you factor in the difference between the minimum insurance required by law on a car and the full coverage required by the lien holder, you end up paying thousands of dollars more in insurance just because you didn't buy the car with cash! Think of it, a $5,000 car could easily end up costing you $15,000 in the long run just because of interest and insurance!

The news isn't all bad, thankfully. Each of the above expenses can either be minimized or used in our favor as well. I had already mentioned that your long-term goal should be to reduce your earned income in favor of passive income, which has the benefit of significantly reducing your legal tax burden. When you own assets like real estate or businesses, you can actually *benefit* from inflation, since it will appreciate the value of your properties and whatever services your company provides. As interest rates increase, any money you lend (in the form of Certificates of Deposit, bonds, or private lending) will end up generate more returns. Insurance can even benefit you if you are using it to protect your assets against damage. For instance, if you have a rental property and a tenant damages it, your insurance coverage can offset the expense of the repairs.

To summarize the Income Statement portion of a Financial Statement, the primary objectives to move toward a life of abundance are:

1. Continually reduce the total percentage of your monthly cash-flow generated by Earned Income
2. Continually increase the total percentage of your monthly cash-flow generated by Portfolio and especially Passive Income
3. Utilize a 10-10-80 rule to control your expenses and facilitate the development of real assets
4. Always factor in the effects of the "four I's" on all your significant financial decisions

The Balance Sheet

If you have ever applied for a home loan from a bank, you have probably had to fill something out that resembles a Balance Sheet. It's basically just a listing of all your assets and liabilities (which is another term for debts.) The bank wants to know these items because they use it to find out what your "debt to income ratio" is, which is the percentage of your income that is already being consumed by credit loans. There is a significant difference between how you would fill out a bank application and your actual Balance Sheet, however, and it has to do with one of the most important lessons I want to convey in this book. It is absolutely imperative that you understand how to tell the difference between an asset and a liability! Conventional methodologies count many things that are actually liabilities as assets. **The determining factor between an asset and a liability is its net effect on your overall cash-flow**. If something you own has a net positive gain at the end of the day, it can be considered an asset. If, however, something you own regularly takes money out of your control without giving it back to you with a return, then it should be considered a liability. This is contrary to traditional financial advice, which says that all those motorcycle, car, and plasma TV purchases are considered assets because you could sell those items if need be. The truth is, each item costs you money regularly (in the form of fuel, electricity, and repairs), without ever adding anything to your actual net cash-flow. Assuming you could sell them, you would never even get the same amount back that you originally paid for them anyway. Adopting this more accurate view of the difference between an asset and a liability will go a long way toward helping you spend your money more wisely. One other point I would like to make is that **many things can be counted as either an asset or a liability depending on how they are used**. For instance, a vehicle by default would be a liability, unless of course you used it as a taxi that generates regular income from its fares. Likewise, if you own the house you live in, it could be considered a liability unless you rented it (or some of its rooms) out to someone else for more than your mortgage payment. Once again, it is how we think that determines our financial situation. My favorite line in the book The Richest Man in Babylon is that "money comes easily to those who understand the laws which govern its acquisition."

The Asset portion of a Balance Sheet can actually be broken up into 4 separate classes:

- REAL ESTATE ASSET CLASS
- PORTFOLIO ASSET CLASS
- BUSINESS ASSET CLASS
- ROYALTY ASSET CLASS

The Real Estate Asset Class consists of any properties owned that generate a net positive cash-flow on a regular basis. This would include rental houses, apartment complexes, parking lots, or commercial properties that businesses pay you to use. It is this class of asset that most affluent individuals hold their wealth in, because of its long-term appreciation and stability.

The Portfolio Asset Class would include any securities owned that generate a regular dividend or capital gain. While it may be easy to simply assume that any stocks you own would fall into this category, keep in mind that if a security has a negative trend to it, then it is no longer an asset and is effectively costing you money. Similarly, if you buy a stock because you expect its value to increase can be likened to gambling, as opposed to choosing one that has historically proven to provide consistent dividends. Something else to keep in mind is that the mentality of "buy, hold, diversify" was invented as a sales pitch to get noninvestors to start putting their money into a stock market they really didn't understand. A better mantra to follow would be something along the lines of "research, buy, and hold as long as it remains an asset." Some traditional examples of securities that can be classified as assets would be high-yield stocks (like Real Estate Investment Trusts), CDs (Certificates of Deposit), or Bonds. Just make sure that you can realize a decent return if you want to stay ahead of inflation!

The Business Class of assets would be any full or partial ownership one has in a company that is generating a consistent profit that it shares with the owners. While a sole proprietorship with just one employee (the owner) would technically qualify as a business asset, ideally the company should have the ability to continue to produce profits without the owner's direct involvement. A self-employed person really just owns a job when you think about it. If the owner stopped working, the money would stop coming in, just like it would if they quit a job. More appropriate examples of a business class asset would be a network marketing company or an automated business like a Laundromat, car wash, or parking garage. Other traditional business models would certainly qualify, as long as you develop them into systems that can be operated by others.

The Royalty Asset Class includes the fees paid to individuals who own intellectual property (IP), like musicians or authors. Creating these residual incomes almost always requires some kind of up-front investment, like publishing costs or recording studio time. Once the IP's ownership is established using a patent or copyright, however, a portion of all the profits generated by it is paid to the owner. If you haven't noticed the trend, each asset class requires a significant up-front investment of time, energy, and money (which is another reason why most people never do any of the things discussed here), but each one has far more earning potential (sometimes unlimited) than simply trading those commodities for an hourly wage, which always has a finite earning potential. All it takes is a simple change in habits away from one mode of thinking toward the other to completely alter the course of one's financial future!

Moving over to the Liabilities portion of the Balance Sheet, there is really only one thing to remember when it comes to debt in general- there are such things as "good" debt and "bad" debt. Once again, how it affects your net cash-flow is what makes the difference. If a mortgage you take out is used to purchase an apartment complex that generates more monthly income than it takes to pay the monthly loan payment, it would be considered a "good" debt. If, on the other hand, you take out a loan to go on a European vacation, that loan would be considered a "bad" debt (unless of course you used that time to meet with a local business owner and set up a partnership that ended up generating significant positive cash-flow for you.) **Just remember that nothing is inherently good or bad in this world; it all depends on how you use it!**

Now that we've taken a brief look at each of the components that make up a Financial Statement, I want to paint a picture of how each part affects your overall financial standing. I'm going to use an analogy of swimming in a flowing river to illustrate my point. If you imagine yourself swimming in that river, there are four different forces at work on you at any given time. Gravity is constantly pulling you down toward a watery grave, while your efforts to tread water keep you afloat. Likewise, the river's current is constantly pushing you backwards, toward a waterfall in the distance, and it is only by your additional expenditure of energy (above and beyond that needed to tread water) that can keep you from going with the flow and falling off the cliff. With that image firmly set in your mind, let me explain what each part represents. The force of gravity is like the constant costs of living in this world (food, fuel, electricity, etc.) that we call our "expenses." The energy expended to "stay afloat" and counteract this force is our regular income (from working at a job.) The current that we all must face in our society is the rampant debt that is almost impossible to avoid, combined with the "Four I's" I talked about earlier in the chapter. The waterfall could easily represent where our working years end and our retirement years begin. Lastly, the additional effort (above and beyond our job) that keeps us away from the sudden drop of the waterfall represents the assets we have accumulated. If enough effort is spent in the development of these assets, one need not fear their retirement years. For at some point, the forward momentum generated by one's wealth will counteract the current and eventually overcome it. Just be careful not to confuse action with motion! Jumping from job to job won't do anything but keep you treading water. You must move forward as well. An old quote from Albert Einstein says it best: "Life is like riding a bicycle- in order to keep your balance, you need to keep moving forward!" As you make large financial decisions going forward, picture the diagram on the next page and ask yourself "will this decision move my family's financial security forward, backward, or just keep us afloat?"

A final thought I would like to leave with you is this: the time, energy, and monetary resources that the Lord has given to all of us can be likened to seeds. As such, they can only be used in three fundamental ways:

1. They can be consumed for our own immediate gratification
2. They can be exchanged for another resource, or
3. They can be planted, watered, and allowed to grow and

produce a harvest far beyond the initial investment

It is my sincere hope that the information shared within these pages has given you a new outlook toward earthly wealth. As long as you invest your resources into building the Lord's kingdom first, and act shrewdly with what he has trusted you with, I am convinced that the Lord will invest his energy in building your family's kingdom here on Earth! Remember, this is only the beginning of your path to abundant living...

Suggestions for Further Reading:

Rich Dad Poor Dad by Robert Kiyosaki

The Cash Flow Quadrant by Robert Kiyosaki

Think and Grow Rich by Napoleon Hill

Grow Rich While You Sleep by Ben Sweetland

Who Moved My Cheese? by Spencer Johnson

The Richest Man in Babylon by George Clason

As a Man Thinketh by James Allen

The Magic of Thinking Big by David Schwartz

The 7 Habits of Highly Effective People by Stephen Covey

The Millionaire Next Door by Thomas Stanley

Twelve Pillars by Jim Rohn

ASSET vs. LIABILITY EXERCISE

For each item, make a note of whether it should be classified as an asset or a liability:

Asset	Liability	
——	——	Money in a savings account
——	——	A house that you own and live in
——	——	A car that you drive for personal use
——	——	A house that you rent for a monthly profit
——	——	A high-yield stock
——	——	Your time
——	——	Credit card debt
——	——	A computer program you write and sell online
——	——	A school loan
——	——	A part-time business
——	——	An ATV (4-wheeler)
——	——	A boat
——	——	A book that you write and sell online
——	——	A timeshare that you and your family use
——	——	A jet ski
——	——	A patent on an invention
——	——	Your financial education
——	——	Gold and Silver
——	——	A Plasma TV

Answers: A, L, L, A, A, A, L, A, L, A, L, L, A, L, L, A, A, A, L

SAMPLE HOUSEHOLD FINANCIAL STATEMENT:

INCOME		EXPENSES	
Earned:		Rent............................$900	
Paycheck......................$2500		Car Payment..................$300	
Portfolio:		Insurance.......................$100	
Dividends........................$100		Food/Clothing................$500	
Passive:		Utilities...........................$200	
Rental Income................$500		Tithe (Income/10)...........$320	
Patent Royalties..............$100		TOTAL:.........................$2320	
TOTAL:..........................$3200			
ASSETS		LIABILITIES	
Stock Value....................$7500		Car Loan....................$10,000	
Patent Costs...................$1000		Credit Card..................$3000	
Rental Real Estate Value........$200,000		Rental Mortgage.........$150,000	
TOTAL:......................$208,500		TOTAL:....................$163,000	

Monthly Cash-Flow (Income minus Expenses): $880

Actual Net Worth (Real Assets minus Liabilities): $45,500

LEAVE A 1-CLICK REVIEW!

Customer Reviews

★★★★★ 15
5.0 out of 5 stars

5 star	▓▓▓▓▓ 100%	Share your thoughts with other customers
4 star	0%	
3 star	0%	Write a customer review
2 star	0%	
1 star	0%	

I would be incredibly grateful if you could take just a minute to write a brief review on Amazon and/or Audible, even if it's just a sentence or two!

www.ingramcontent.com/pod-product-compliance
Lightning Source LLC
Chambersburg PA
CBHW030502220526
45464CB00006B/2618